waterwa

Deluge

releasing new voices, revealing new perspectives

Deluge

waterways
a poetry series of flipped eye publishing
www.flippedeye.net

First Edition
Copyright © Charlotte Ansell, 2019
Cover Concept & Finishing © flipped eye publishing, 2017, 2019
Cover Letter Typeface Design & Front Layout © D237, 2017 | www.d237.com

Charlotte Ansell would like to thank the editors and judges of the following publications, productions and competitions, where versions of of some of the poems in this collection first appeared: Mslexia Poetry Competition, Poems on the Trams-Imove, Fire Anthology, Butcher's Dog, The Sheffield Anthology, Poetry Review, Loose Muse Anthology, 'The very best of 52' Anthology, Apples and Snakes Podcast, Sheffield Poetry TV, Now Then, Ground, Picaroon, Prole, WordLife Anthology, Clear Poetry, Obsessed with Pipework, Frogmore Press Anthology, Verse Matters Anthology and Algebra of Owls; as well as any other journals that have supported her work. *Emptied* won first prize in the Red Shed Open Poetry Competition in 2015.; *Facultative Symbionts* was a finalist in the 2015 Fun Palaces BBC Write Science Competition and *Containment* won first prize in the Watermarks Poetry Competition in 2016.

ISBN: 978-1-905233-55-7

For Sean who keeps me afloat - always metaphorically, sometimes literally as well and my girls who don't look like they will grow into great lovers of poetry anytime soon but have their own passions to make me proud.

Deluge

Acknowledgements

Very many thanks to the poetry villages I have been lucky enough to be part of; most importantly Nii Parkes, Jacob Sam-La Rose, Niall O'Sullivan and all the flipped eye family; Malika Booker's Poetry Kitchen; Thea Poets; Jo Bell's (ably supported by Norman Hadley) immense 52 project, where some of these poems were born); Joe Kriss & Wordlife; Ray Hearne and Matt Black at Writing Yorkshire; Gram Joel Davies' Critical Bathtub; Gav Robert's ROMP in Rotherham and the Facebook 30/30 group.

To the poets, friends and poet-friends who gave invaluable critique, support and feedback: heartfelt thanks to Janett Plummer, Be Manzini, Abe Gibson, Agnes Meadows, Roger Robinson, Rachel Bower, Claire Collinson, Stella Wulf, Kate Forsyth, Anna Spedding, Wendy Pratt and everyone else along the way who unwittingly or otherwise provided inspiration and love – I hope you find nothing in these pages to cause offence.

Special thanks to my long time muse and closest friend, Jennie McShannon.

And to you – whoever you are – thanks for reading. A poem is only really born when it's been read.

Deluge

Contents

Drizzle

Queen of the North

Oh my God Sheffield why
do you always leave your coat at home?
bare shouldered
and hard, you'd wear your heart on sleeves
if you had them, though you'd rather swagger
in your Santa hat
and leopard skin top, shivering on corners
with a fag. Your dreams are not in tatters

but lacquered into your big hair,
your mascara however much it's run,
you're all bluff
and front, as you sail on, invincible,
truculent and pissed, insist your chips
are in vinegar
not on your shoulder, you snigger
at the nesh southerner on the bus wrapped

in four layers, a cardi and a scarf.
Sheffield you old tart, either shouting the odds
or a mardy bum
sulking into a shot glass, late home down ginnels
brushing away tears you carry on regardless,
even your canal
tinkles with a brittle, forced laugh,
burdened by your jewellery, the metallic glint

and wink of cars. You never let anyone into
your steely heart, you spew up your guts
from pubs and bars,
your glitter eye shadow is street lights

smudging into puddles, your neon nails
punctuating the darkness, weaving drunkenly
through a prickle of stars, your bravado
stilettos staccato on pavements.

The Handkerchief

Rain smacks the windows so hard it ought to leave scars
like welts on the underside of the sky,
but inside's a cheery glow. We're snuggled into coats
with the Hillsborough lads who'll be
Wednesday 'til they die, whatever the score.
My kids smile, bug-eyed, clutching in tight fingers
blank tickets the conductor gave with a wink.
Spare hands grasp mine; tacit reminders I'm not alone.
"Love you too" a man snaps off his phone, rolls his eyes
"soft as a sofa that one" he grins. We have pulled away
from Perseverance Terrace towards home,
and the girl I was, one wasted night,
wearing pain like a neon dress, slips into the dark.

I couldn't have known, that the stranger
who insisted I kept
a crisp white square
with her initial embroidered in blue,
who held my hand through all London's bleak stops
would be more memorable now
than the man I'd loved
whose name might as well be Judas.
There's always a time to choose;
like the girl (who is no longer me)
left Battersea, moved north.
Now the rain quietens
as the sky clears,
closer here to Sunnyside,
the distance travelled is eighteen years.

Flat Caps and Ferrets

We bring our London ways north
suspicious of the stranger on the towpath
who asks: *Are we settling in alright?*
my head in a book on the train,
not joining in the chat
thinking; surely these women
can't have just met?
The chippy sells spam fritters
mushy peas, cheesy chips,
but I miss the saveloys, a fortune cookie
'for the kiddie' from our East End Chinese,
miss *'Alright mate?'* and *'See ya'*
now it's *'Ay up'* and *'Ta- ra'*.
At the gym the sign on the door
says *'Outdoor shoes not to be wore in studio'*
our tongues twist round unwieldy vowels.

We arrived the weekend
the Tinsley Towers came down
Sheffield sodden, stolid
not the style over substance we left behind;
yummy mummies with designer buggies
Shoreditch boys on Vespas
Brick Lane dandies, barely dressed.
Here admiration would be replaced by mutters:
'Daft buggers.'
A cliché of obligatory steel and Hovis
open die forgings, seamless rings,
trading the Isle of Dogs and Bethnal Green
for Brightside, Attercliffe.
Scrawled in the dust of a back door:

'Nobody's lass is more filthy than this van'
sounds better than:
'I wish me wife was this dirty'
averted eyes on the tube,
the under the breath dis,
sadly, it's the hostility I miss.

I drive out of Leeds,
take the M1 lane signposted
Wakefield, London,
like a carrot, a promise
dangling on a string.
I wonder if I might just keep going.
200 miles south. So far.
Why did we leave behind
the place we loved?
A better life for our children?
Seeking our fortune
in this pitted landscape
of grit and muck and rain,
common sense and straight talking,
of dinner for lunch
tea for dinner,
of steel slag heaps, Mother's Unions,
Sally Army brass bands and bingo halls
but so little I can call
familiar.

Ode to Sheffield

If you're doing nowt, meet me at the fountain,
we'll skulk in the tropics of the Winter Gardens,

listen to the fans go hoarse at Bramall Lane,
ride the tram to Halfway and back again.

Chapeltown, Hillsborough, Gleadless, Malin Bridge,
Grenoside, Greystones, Shalesmoor, Attercliffe.

We'll see sunlight slant off slate grey stone,
ancient woodland blanket round terraced homes.

We'll watch a Magic Lantern film, eat pies in Sharrow,
tea at the Rude Shipyard, go to Padley Gorge; paddle.

Rivelin Valley, Millhouses Park, Eccesall Woods,
Forge Dam, Nether Edge, Heeley City Farm, Crookes.

We'll scour Division Street for tat and vintage dresses,
hang out in Cole Brothers, loiter in Lowedges,

take the kids to swim in rings at Pond's Forge,
window shop on Abbeydale for furniture we can't afford.

Burngreave, Stannington, Brightside, Dore
Atlas, Manor Top, Ecclesfield, Pitsmoor.

Pinpoints of light glance off the canal, a towering wheel,
rough- hewn edges, a centre of glass, mirrors, steel.

And when we're all worn out and the day is at an end,
we'll salute you Sheffield, in all your shabby glory, a friend.

Knife

This knife is Sheffield born
out of the streams, stones
and tors of the Peaks,
the girth and heft of Stannage Edge,
shank with the sever sharp cut
of the grass on Blacka Moor.

Take a knife like this,
crafted gently from Sheffield steel,
handle of giraffe shin or mammoth tusk
that asks respect.

A knife that's proud,
cutler's signature exactly rendered
by hand and file
that won't be cowed,
descended from Vikings,
Damascus pattern welded
knowing strength is in the join;
hardness at the edge,
resistance in the blade
whorls that carry pain.

So if you should say goodbye
to these seven hills,
take this knife as leaving gift
pay for it with a penny,
taking no risks,
grip decision in your hands
curl your fingers around the haft.

Because the heart is no match for a knife,
and this was no second chance
just another false start
when what's torn cannot be stitched
without leaving a seam,
ruptures can not always be healed;
if you scrape or shave these doubts,
be sure the wound is clean.

Lacerate all ties,
breathe this high clarity of air
above the coughed up city
the steel that weighs you down
mundane and too solid,
go without turning
in one fell stab, shock and thrust,
ignore the ache you cradle,
jagged edged and raw,
as you walk away from the town
that was never yours.

Rainbows

Jennie

You meet me from the tube,
bare feet, impossibly micro
shorts, pixie hair. *'You
could still be seventeen...*

in the dark' I say,
dodging your shove.

As if we could peel away
the years like flaky skin, go
back to the cold weather shelter work;
your nearly indecipherable
Belfast vowels, penchant for denim
and that prick, who scrunched you
into a ball until you rolled
out from under to waltz down
Brixton High St with the gentle Italian
you couldn't love
but who wouldn't break you.

Not much could; incorrigible grin
and mischief, those obscene
vulva-toed boots you bought,
the time you met Prince Charles,
gave him your business card with a wink;
queen of the faux pas, regaling
any room with your tales – that laugh!

Still all eyes and legs at forty two,
talking faster than the boil of the expresso pot,
our time together in meagre slices now,

not the weekend slabs we used to have
that even then weren't enough.

You come in for a wee
while I clean my teeth;
I'm trying to digest your news –
the Brighton house you've put an offer on.
After fourteen years of making sofa cushions
into a bed on your living room floor,
in the house that watched us grow up.

I let myself out at five am, walk
into the subdued pale of a Tottenham
morning, tell myself a few hundred
miles more won't hurt.
Remind myself
I've always loved the sea.

In Praise of Us

When we puffed away
the dandelion days of youth:
Darren, all camp six foot of him,
wolf-whistling builders
on scaffolding from his bike;
Jennie graffiti-bombing Brixton
with hearts and flowers, peace signs.

The smoke rings, conversations
that hung in the air,
the booths and powder rooms
at the Rivoli before retro was cool,
the queue for chips after.
Michelle leaving answer phone messages
for the cats at our Vauxhall flat,
hopeless as letters carved
in wet sand on the beach.

In praise of making pennies
last for weeks when nothing else did,
vaulting the gates into Greenwich Park,
stargazing, pints downed too fast,
Victor laughing that enthusiasm
was my only grace at African Dance,
the tangled limbs, the heart to hearts
'til morning frayed the edges
of a faded Levi's sky,
the sweaty bumping of bodies at *Mass*,
drugs and fiddle playing at Matt's,
the craic, when we threw our beauty
like rags to men who didn't deserve it.

When we didn't know
freedom was like champagne,
too long and you forget the taste;
the days before we were
weighed down by children,
squandering entire weekends,
those boat trips up the Thames;
those dreams when we were dragonflies,
for who we were when
we had no clue what we had,
for all that's gone,
and what we hold on to now,
indelible as a song.

Love Song to London During the World Cup

In this house which is no longer their house
with their children who are not my children
in the town which I can no longer call home
(now I notice how rank the water tastes in tea)
I lie here listening to her Belfast tones
and his drawl, reaching me two floors below
stretched out on the living room floor
with the cat disconsolately pushing her bowl –
the clink, scrunch and crunch
as she nudges the dried up remains.
The dishwasher pushes into my thoughts
with its don't-think numbing swish and swirl
tumble and fall, as just one mosquito
circles in a whine of wanting,
my head stuffed full
of all your irritating ways.

Earlier, as Ghana scored
and they both screamed,
jumping involuntarily to their feet
as, through the open patio doors,
a corresponding roar of pipe dreams
reached us from the other side of the park,
I remembered
how tantalising you always were.
You were subdued on Thursday as England
failed to perform again and I too was chastened,
a jealous ex who can't quite turn away
after six long years.
I wouldn't mind
but you haven't even noticed I've gone.

The Girls Who Birthed Us

We bring them with us though they don't behave,
have smeared their names in lipstick on the mirrors,
dug out the gold lamé and sequins, the awkward heels,
they trail after us with squeals and smirks.

Back at yours, they've eaten all the chocolate you stashed,
the Turkish bread we'd saved for breakfast,
necked the wine. When we turn in we still hear them,
chaining chatter, stubbing out cigs,
candles bitten to the wicks like their fingernails.

As we nurse morning mugs of tea,
their giggles echo our conversation,
knees drawn up on the windowsill,
kitten eyes wider than their yawns.

Sometimes I see their breath mist
behind us as we walk the canal,
they hug to themselves armfuls of leaves
rifled from piles of flame, of gold;
plunder for an art school collage.

On Sundays, they offer to take the kids,
trying on motherhood for the fit
like dresses they can't afford,
they bend and kiss dimpled cheeks,
pointedly push swings like the louche boys
hanging off their bikes are invisible,
signalling with the subtlety of baboons
they could be suitable wives.

Last week they flashed a bit of cleavage
for extra points in the pub quiz
but would never call it flirting,
always insist on changing
their own tyres, washers, plugs.

They lug home stacks of worthy books
they will read less than half of,
abandoning *Das Kapital* (though they did try).
They tire in the end and we tuck them in,
smooth stray curls behind their ears,
caress their cheeks,
leave them to dream.

Document

Naked save for a wedding ring,
this account is not oral or written
but lived, my story within

and on the surface
of a no longer blank sheet;
etched, scratched, screwed up, torn,

scribed, smudged, worn
and stretched: tiny traumas and hurts,
the absolution of births,

the creep towards a fading script.

These shoulders stitch the weight
of pages, arms bookmark
all the chapters hidden inside.

In the title lines of bones
beneath my neck, youth is still
an indent, but ages

into a dense paragraph of breasts,
the trace of babies' indulgence
in the scribbled folds of what was

my waist. My knees and shins scored

with crossed-through arguments
of cycle accidents, bramble scars,
football wounds; scabbed still

and bruised like a child's.
This document is fiercely
mine - and his; a poem

with an audience of one.

Starstruck

My sister spent the seventies
in a Wonder Woman costume,
or that mud brown jumpsuit
draped over Dad's Cortina for a photo,
tossing hair that cascaded
in glossy waves.

She could have passed,
for a glamorous extra
in Starksy and Hutch
but she held no truck with romance
snorted at adverts for diamonds.

Her wedding present
from Clay, her husband,
was a binary star,
a promise
that he would
eternally orbit
her brilliance.

She divorced him.

In another galaxy far away,
his celestial version still circles,
while she has settled
for her slippers, pjs
and TV reruns with corny detectives.

Facultative Symbionts*

We were never two peas in a pod,
our paths forked early; hers to colonising
the linen cupboard with fruit flies during school,
progressing through trypanosomes and HIV,

double-gloved in negative pressure laboratories,
to the schistosomiasis she calls beautiful,
its so romantic how the female has
a groove the male snuggles in for life.

She keeps a Bristol Stool sample chart
taped to the fridge, doesn't think it odd
and while it's alien to me
her fascination with poo and bugs,

she's conversing with the divine,
the way life intertwines, the tiny cells
that form tissues that build
into complex organs, how we all connect,

and parasites like *Dicrocoelium dendriticum*
complete their life cycle by
performing mind control on ants,
making them climb the tallest grass

---

* facultative symbiont – symbiont from the state of symbiosis meaning the living together
of two dissimilar organisms in more or less intimate association or close union. Facultative
meaning 'optional' or 'discretionary' in reference to a symbiotic relationship, as in they
can live together successfully or apart.

so they're eaten by ruminants.
We all need each other; after all,
this girl who speaks a different language
shared a host, a womb with me.

But we are both obsessed with insides;
for me it's minds; like why she chose biology,
focussed on Mr Ennion's belief in her
and ignored Mr Curtis' provocative *girls can't.*

Her eyes spark bright as the glow worms we saw
on the Waikato River when she remembers
her own malaria parasites under a lens in Africa,
these nematodes and trematodes she loves,

the diseases she succumbed to for science
were worth nearly dying for.
Her world is both tiny and vast.
Do you know we are more bacterial than human?

She whispers with awe, not disgust.

A Little Scrap of Nowhere

If there is the rasp of bicycle wheels
along the towpath
like the drone of wasps;
if there are the high pitched
squeals and bumps
of the children on the trampoline,
cat indolent in the only patch
of sun on the back deck;
if the air is heavy with the conflict
of lavender, rosemary and diesel,
the canal a thick curtain
of green velvet thrown across
to disguise the jagged
broken bottle edges
of the scrapyard walls;
if the messy strain of the day
has been left at the gates,
if you can shrug it off your shoulders
sitting lazy and undone
as the sun blooms tea roses into the sky
reflected as bruised, fallen petals
in the water.

If no one has yet demanded
your attention or mentioned dinner
and you can pretend,
it's so easy here to be
on holiday from the world beyond;
if the other boats hug the bankside
like fat slugs and there is a patchwork
of noisy love, scrambled hugs and chatter,

a stretch of ripples, sky and dreaming,
the sun nuzzling your neck,
then you will know how lucky you are
to claim this little scrap of nowhere
as home.

My England met yours

last night, on my way to a party,
the pavement piled high with boxes
of Pakistani mangoes, Arabian coffee
houses nestled in a pick and mix
of takeaways, arriving to a house full of kids
who didn't care about who's from where,
as they minced around the lounge,
wine glasses aloft,
feet adrift in their mother's heels.

My England met yours last night
with mixed results;
the Spanish neighbour and his boyfriend
said the old lady next door spat
over the fence no matter how often
they offered to mow her lawn
or took round home-baked bread.
They sat here laughing with the Derry girls
who found they loved each other
more than men.

And the Polish man in the kitchen,
expounding on how he is applying ideas
from Eric Fromm to architecture,
and the most important thing
he can teach his students is freedom.
My England met yours when I left at 3am,
a weary middle-aged white woman,
colliding with Muslims heading for mosque
to pray before they fast.

This night in the backyard,
the bodhran struck tentative beats,
the pipe threw hopeful notes
into the air like birds,
warmed by the chiminea's sparks,
how we all wanted to sing together
and it didn't matter
that none of us quite knew all the words.

Jumping Puddles

Looking for Crocodiles

This is the river that looked so calm until she stepped in
because she was tired and closed her eyes on Halloween
when all the gauze of her witch's costume fanned around and held her up
(or the time before when she was looking for crocodiles)

And this is the call from school on the first day back
When I believed, *"there's no need to panic, she's absolutely fine..."*
to arrive and find a tooth knocked through her lip
where she'd fallen off the climbing frame.

While this is the open hinge of the safety pin, perfectly picked out,
sitting bone white inside her stomach back-lit on the X-ray slide,
that soured her dad's marathon triumph,
after she swallowed it just to see *"what it tasted like"*.

Or this the gap between the old diesel tank and the wall
with the frog and mucky puddle where she got trapped
when she somersaulted down the bank unseen while we tried
in vain to work out where she'd fallen, from her screams.

And the hospital that couldn't find any cause at a week old
despite her temperature rising to 104, the lumbar puncture,
the endless tests, the lack of rest or any kind of peace,
with not even a cup of tea allowed on the children's ward.

This the day that she was born when nothing
foreshadowed the path ahead, when she slid out
within an hour or so, no pain relief, this dream birth,
this elfin girl, who ever since has made us beg,

for ordinary.

Spoon Fed

Her early days we keep in a drawer,
with her first snipped curl,
each tooth lost to fairies,
the wayward slope of run on letters:
ones pon tim...

Between the folds of Baby-gros
are echoes of innocence and measure,
a time of sips, when everything was
as simple as aeroplane deliveries,
as easily read as a turned head or parted lips,

a belief that tiny mouthfuls
could be the answer to any trouble,
soothing as medicine, porridge,
soup, fed on hope
that comes smooth not choked.

And nestled in a hug of velvet,
cribbed in a box,
a silver egg cup and christening spoon,
her name engraved down the handle,
now a little worn.

She wasn't born with this in her mouth;
these gifts came later,
the way she learnt to wait,
to anticipate the nipple, the teat,
each small steel bowl.

Emptied

I didn't feel you slip away,
cocooned I waited
for proof on a screen.

You were there alright,
my nearly child
but the probe was

as silent as snow,
no heartbeat thrum
of horse's hooves,

leaving me to face
alone the vicissitudes
of the nurse

who scolded me
for my emerald varnished toes
that apparently I should

have scraped clean
before the surgeon in her ice
white box of theatre,

scraped me clean of you.
I left vacuumed, numb;
nothing to show or keep,

no fuzzy blizzard shot
of obscured head and tiny feet,
no blood-stained sheets,

no memento
to stave off the aftermath;
your dad's brash sister

with her usual tact,
saying a fortune teller told her
you would have been a boy.

Wound

I will remember this night in pieces:
the glass as it shattered, the moment
when her chatter was drowned out
by a thud, the splattering of tight sharp shards,
that endless pause before she howled,
how just feet away we all tried to run
and I scooped her out of her auntie's arms,
seeing the too bright, too large drops of blood,
not knowing where they stemmed from,
looking first at her knees,
prising at her fingers as she still screamed
and her dad pulled back her sleeve,
dropping it immediately
"Jesus- call an ambulance!"
panic sounding like anger.
I looked again at the wide wound
that etched a tattoo on my brain,
replayed in flashbacks through the night,
all of the next day,
how I held her wrist so tight,
her arm above her head
to slow the sickening tide of red
as my other daughter backed away sobbing,
I held out my spare arm to her
but she wouldn't come,
she wouldn't come.
I will hear like a jerky soundtrack,
the staccato words as her uncle dialled 999,
as I held her close, close,
kissed her face, wrapped strips of wipes
around her tiny wrist,

tried to keep the flaps of skin together.
I will remember my own arm dead
from holding hers aloft,
that nothing would possess me to let it fall,
from within a towel
the hugeness of her wide blue eyes,
a silence that she'd never had before
no words, not even a nod of response
just huddled in – in shock.

At the hospital
the blinding insistence of the lights,
the kindness of the nurse,
the picture on the wall that caught my eye,
though I wished it hadn't;
of a smiling boy
with two dates – not one – underneath,
23.02.03- 07.04.05.
Appalled I turned away
from what could so nearly
have been my child,
immortalised.

Paw

This small creature is heart-warm
wilful and not to be refused;
it knows what it wants.

It scrabbles, pulsed with sweat,
its markings felt tip stains,
grubbed earth. A quiet grasp

of limbs that end
in baby crescents, not
luminescent but sticky arcs.

It is a mole emerging blind
from a woven hole
while its sister stays out

with a thumb almost
permanently stoppered
to their owner's mouth.

I like it best on the walk to school,
when it crawls into my own hand
and we both hold fast.

the love heart fairy

Just six; all eyes in a pixie shaped face,
a gold cascade Rumplestiltskin would covet,
spindly legs clumsy as a newborn foal's,
words tumble in cadences of shriek to shout.

She conjures her character
in a costume chiefly consisting of
in-your-face pink; fluorescent and bold.
She tells anyone who will listen

"I am the love heart fairy
my role is spreading love"
with sticky-out wings,
flower lei around her neck,

feathers tucked peacocky into her skirt
her cheeks striped with paint
she holds court, self-appointed queen
under the magic tree.

Here conventional kids look odd,
bohemia reigns beneath stars and saris
ticky-tackeyed up in branches,
beardy men on unicycles,

big kids on space hoppers,
mummies wearing babies like blankets,
swirly patterns, spicy tea,
solar panels, pakoras, crochet.

She voices disgust at organic bean wraps,
no ketchup? or burgers in sight
as the happy crowd twirl into the night,
carefree 'til morning.

In this spirit of free love,
a stranger asks me to mind her child
while she takes her baby to her tent.

The next day, only those too wired
to sleep are left, as our heroine rises
to continue her love mission,
and a wasted crocodile runs in circles.

He spots her, affably tries to push her swing
but she screams *"Get off! GET. OFF. MEEEEE!"*
jumps off, feet planted, hands on hips:
a pout, knotted eyebrows, flint sharp eyes.

I watch, proud of her defiance, her city girl cheek,
as the crocodile deflates and goes.
Even a love heart fairy must be clear:
sometimes it will be necessary to say *No.*

Minus the Miracle Birth

It's for the best you didn't come
the other mums never know what to say.

Mrs B chants *Good Aft-ter-noon Ev-rey-one.*
The kids intone it back,
it's standing room only now.

At home you nurse a cuppa,
keep the curtains drawn,
imagine a shadow entering centre-stage,
a faint giggle, the swish of a ponytail.

Seven years of tears
leak into your womb,
as you count up
all the birthdays, Christmases',
Harvest assemblies, Nativities,
the pennies that weren't needed
for leotards, swim costumes,
fancy dress, football kit or ballet shoes.

There'll be no trips to charity shops
with outgrown clothes and books,
no Star of the Week certificates
pinned to your fridge,
no pencilled height marks
scaling the cupboard door,
no felt tip stains
you can't scrub off the walls.

Your boast is to drink your tea
before it goes cold,
to pee without an audience.

What you'd give
to be ushered into the school hall,
to sit and smile until your face aches,
one pair of eyes searching for yours.

Umbrellas and Lifeboats

What You Learned in Therapy

That hours are not elastic,
your mind is a colander
letting the happy drain away
while the dregs are stubborn, stay in place.
Mistakes are not seams that can be
unpicked but defiant stains.

That many doors won't open
and those that do, will not always
lead to rooms you want to be in.
You will always ride a see-saw through
despair; hope is as fragile as eggshells
but sometimes holds.

That chess is won in the middle game;
those battles determine the result.
When it seems life is passing you by
is when it matters most.

That autistic traits protect like armour;
sometimes alone is the safest place.

That it doesn't often feel like it's
the trying or taking part that counts
but winning is like grasping
a balloon that will deflate;
success will fade, like new clothes
too many times washed.

That the poem you write today
is not the poem you'll write
tomorrow or next week;
talk isn't cheap; listening will,
like woollen socks, trump
a fancy bra that digs into flesh.

That you don't feel as broken
as these words suggest,
you're just so tired of trying;
the child who felt awkward
hasn't disappeared,
you are not wiser only more battered.

That there will always be
winners and losers
and mostly you aren't either;
the end is neither far away nor near.

The trick is to remember
you're here though, you're still here.

At ten thirty every Thursday,

we meet in this room.
He is six,
wears hidden scars
like an electric fence;
Don't look at me! Don't talk!
He piles furniture into the doll's house,
builds the backdrop to a horror film,
stacks Playmobil figures
into the aftermath of a massacre,
runs the ambulance over a child.
The paramedics and policemen are zombies,
the mummy morphs into a robot,
the daddy isn't here.
Have you got kids?
Tell me, tell me you fucking bitch!

He kicks his shoes off towards my face,
squeezes paint all over the carpet,
smears spit across the window panes
before giving teddy medicine and a hug.
We have an hour.
It's not enough.

Phoenix

This is the boy
who grew up
believing his mum
deserved it,
her crazy like
lighter fuel
to his dad's combust
and explode,
the boy who fell
through the cracks
to don't care, foster homes
and contempt;
who dreamt up
a suicide pact
with his sister at eight,
to drink bleach,
whose picture of family
was so skewed
the Hell's Angels
seemed a better bet,
who ran a man
down at fifteen
because there was
no other way.

This is the boy
who snarled,
coiled like a rusted spring
about to ping back
and snag,
who lived on high alert,

who was the man
who burnt a crater
through what we had,
whose fingers forced
a scorch of red
to choker my neck,
cracked my head
off the wall
as a set of big eyes
looked up from her tea,
her whimper
burning into a scream.

I am the woman who
keeps secrets like a grate
but told the one friend
who would recognise
the restraint he showed.

For this is the man
who may break
the stranglehold
of generations
It's been seven years,
I might stop counting
soon.

Middle: An Assay

Sometimes you're the piggy,
the spare part, the third wheel,
your struggle is mostly Oedipal.

You're always in between,
feeling it's you; grown up too fast,
the child listening from the stairs.

You're the favoured possessions
of mummy bear; the porridge,
the chair, the bed. Goldilocks

didn't want you, no one did.
You are forever overlooked
but always there- except

when you're the empty in a polo,
the dropped stitch, the gap left
when the first baby tooth falls out.

You're the stubborn of *me do it!*
Shoelaces, mouthfuls, tangled curls,
the tantrum in the Tesco's aisle.

You'll become a wish to be
unseen; gawky, gangly, acned,
the ugly before the swan

or the mousey huddle of girls
in school, picked before the fat girl
but never called by your name.

You've had your moments
but you've never won,
you cannot be alone.

You hold it all together;
won't be undone. And damn,
weren't you always the precious one.

Absolution

It's a steep climb up her drive. I suspect
she's wryly aware how apt this feels.

She nods a terse hello, gives a not-quite smile
opens the door enough to let me pass.

She doesn't ask questions or offer tea,
gives the assurances of a priest.

I cannot count the knots on her ceiling or forever read,
furtively, the sideways spines of her books.

she has no interest in nice, instead
she waits for the scum to rise.

I resist the urge to try to amuse,
I know like Freud she won't believe in jokes.

This is not the place
to weigh or consider words,

she leads me down a royal road,
I give her dreams; ah yes, she's keen on those.

some days I'm fighting every sentence,
my life no longer mine, no discrete events,

only those framed by the lens
of her gaze and a couch.

I surrender to the intimacy, lie down,
Isaac to her Abraham.

On Balance

Neither your inside nor
the outside can settle,
in freefall, begging for the safety
of a promise kept, like a kid
in a coat by the front door
on fortnightly weekends,
fingers and toes crossed.
When hope is so much more
treacherous than doubt
the middle child has such
difficulty with the in between;
you talk to yourself, you dream, you stall,
your mind barred windows
and locks – not open playgrounds;
no dimmer switch for thoughts
that won't turn off,
the lurch from rejection
to success and back.
You've lost the stomach for swings,
see-saw through extremes,
you are a sandcastle
when the tide comes in.

You so easily forget that
Spring follows Winter
with no effort on your part,
when pick-up-sticks branches
are the lead to a stained glass sky,
there is no *and*
to make rainbows –
only black or white.

Everything real can rise
or be knocked down
like *Lego* blocks.
You try to find the greys within,
call it progress.

Drained

Drained

There are days
when paint floods the page
like a toddler's masterpiece
exploding more more more!
When God has entered a manic phase,
scatter-gunned with the roar
of an early Technicolor film,
the glare of over-bright.

But my eyes are a reverse prism
stripping everything back to white.
Not holy light but the sun leaching it all to pale;
old dog turds on pavements,
the remains of eggs congealed
in yesterday's pan, knickers
washed to indeterminate drab,
collapsed into absence.

At home, a grubby fingerprinted
sheet pressed in my hands,
on it a shape outlined in black felt tip
and "Mummy your the best!"
expectant faces turned up like sunflowers
smiles, rainbowing the ache.

40

I have shrunk to this; a clod
of my daughter's dirty socks, stuffed
in my bag after last night's karate,

forgotten alongside my roll ups, my phone,
scraps of paper with foetuses of sentences
that will never birth poems.

I dream of attic bedrooms, wide skies,
escape, of student days, dubious
relationships, when at least I knew myself.

That life I mapped in hope is stillborn;
the remains, handfuls of empty
aspirations that never drew breath.

My children like a slack rope
around my neck; if I pull away it tightens.
I couldn't ever love them less
but they are greedy, promise stealers,
chewing up my dreams, my unvoiced regrets
choked down whole.

Impossible contradictions. A hand reaching for mine,
a sleep-heavy hug, a dirty giggle, can
cut through the wreckage with delight.

These best years are a hole I will crawl out of
old; as forty exposes each and every excess
like poverty etches lines in faces,

my body fudged around the edges,
my weaknesses not just on my sleeves,
but in every fold and crease of flesh

that the young shrug off.
They mock old age, too far to be real
while duty shrouds each grain of time,

snatches it away, the grey
around my temples only grows
as colour recedes.

But it is not just these visible signs
that haunt me, nor my children's unwitting fault;
I have made them an excuse

as mediocre creeps from the corner,
the spectre
that can no longer be ignored.

On Envy

It doesn't floor me as a punch
but creeps – a virus that sits
in my stomach, heavy and too solid,
like stones in my pockets,
or a drip down my neck.

It's the smashed plate glass of the
Mercedes Benz showroom,
the screwed up face and clenched fists
of the child who didn't get the sweets
in the Sunday sermon from the priest.

It is a blunt knife
that shaves the edges off the sun,
its putting a contact lens
in the wrong eye
and like swimming,
trouble only comes
when you stay in too long.

Today it seemed
getting round to cleaning
would only seep
resentment into my bones.
Instead I find that making good
the little we have,
shoring up the cracks,
has its own comfort
and picking herbs for dinner
makes me think surely it's God
who is in the detail, with each one
an exact remedy for its own ill.

I haven't found the salve yet,
but sometimes I can say
'Well done, I'm pleased for you'
and mean it.

Fragile

It's the time of year for spiders,
their webs too pretty to be death traps

and who knew weeds would be
a match for paving slabs?

Cycling to work at 8am,
a man outside M & H News,

flails in a Superman dressing gown.
We all have our kryptonite,

our Achilles heel. I pull
myself together with fake cigarettes

and sticking plasters,
pretend I have not laid tissue paper

over an abyss, try to convince myself
if I walk across it will hold.

Sometimes there is precious little
left to dig deep for.

I have mined the last of resources
that were meagre to begin with,

when even prayers feel
like messages in bottles

but still my smile
announces to the world

I am whole, unbreakable,
which I am – of sorts.

In hope,

number 73 have put deckchairs out on South Street,
surveying the Rainbow Car Wash, Akbar's, the sewage works.

Piles of fly tipping are strewn on the verge
like the rummage of a dress-up box.

The sky is soggy, a balled tissue damp with tears;
there are slug trails in the children's shoes.

I don't want them to be like me,
in needle cord flares, laughed at in the playground.

The forecast announces summer
will be back tomorrow; it may not be enough.

The accordion player on the corner in Sharrow,
is discordant with persistence not talent,

wafts of yeast and olives toss seeds of aspiration
from the windows of the Seven Hills Bakery.

In Weston Park, the ducklings have hatched,
furiously paddling to keep up.

A child's ball drops, floats to the middle of the pond.
She wills the wind to bring it back,

waits resolute against her mum's impatience
refusing to budge until it comes.

The way home is unremarked,
deckchairs flapping beneath a cold sun.

At the Bluebird Hairstyling Salon

NOW magazine proclaims: *It's war*
between Jen and Angelina.
Dieting has destroyed your looks
bluebirds flutter round Hollywood bulbs
basking in their fake suns,
the retro lamp, the genteel stacks
of china tea cups; shelved,
the trainee stylist all seeing like an owl,
with those big framed specs
all the young girls wear.
They talk kettle bells, ex-best friends
and getting toned for Ibiza
while I just sit, pretend to read.

She can't find her scissors,
says *I swear there's gremlins in here*
stuff's always getting lost - it's odd,
and it is; when you misplace
something important,
like the girl I met at art college,
with the bluest eyes,
who could lie for England,
who was by turns a hand model
or an international spy,
who glided up to her wedding
to *'Dream a little dream'* in
a boat fashioned into a polystyrene swan
rocking vintage lace, who made
plaster casts of her belly in pregnancy,
giant sunflowers out of crochet,
who saw me through the years

of broken hearts, impermanence and regret
and was so effortlessly more
everything than anyone I'd met
but who no longer buys gifts for my kids
at Christmas, or returns my calls

and is lost to me now,
like the mysterious world of women,
or a pair of scissors that can't be traced,
that has somehow slipped
between another lady's bag and the wall.

Not Ever After

It was our running joke
about who was really your best friend,
Sinead or me; until it wasn't.
Maybe none of our quips were funny,
they might always have been wounds
caused by a barbed forest
guarding a hundred years of sleep.
It's been three years four months
since I heard from you.

My tongue was too often
fast and loose with your treasures.
I thought of you as a sister
in all the wrong ways,
trying to steal your clothes
and who says doors are made
for slamming? Sometimes
you need more than a makeshift curtain,
you can know too much about a person
– and still not enough.

We were going places though, weren't we?
All the must-see destinations;
Helsinki, Pescara, Hull.
We never stalled, gridlocked perhaps
until we drove off in opposite directions,
lost ourselves, with no map or route back
to the years we squandered.

Years like a scratched 45. As flat mates
with our sibling cats, the rooftop sofa chats

under the bruising sighs of the eucalyptus,
the wheelbarrow you insisted
I push you in while you filmed,
your avant-garde skills that begged an audience;

experiments in paint and words
that dissolved us helpless into giggles,
or just helpless; dancing
past the strike of midnight,
you in silver stilettos, me in blue wedges
that might as well have been red.

Those days dead now, though
we're not too grown up or too old,
distanced by more miles than the fifty minute trawl
down the M1 and the arrogance I wore;
at best like an emperor too flattered to be wise,
at worst like the scissors we sliced into dress fabric.
All those designs – only this time
without pattern or purpose.

Dear K,

You showed up in my dreams
in the early hours; no warning as usual,
reminiscent of the time you threatened
to gate-crash my wedding,
playing wicked fairy from Sleeping Beauty,
with slurred words and curses,
If any person here present
knows of any lawful impediment…
You would have stood for sure.
My feelings for you now lean to
fondness, more concern than love;
the after-pub-kicking-out
appearances on my doorstep,
buttons ripped from your shirt,
squinting through a boxer's eye,
trying to piss in my wardrobe, lost
in the disenchanted night, are gone.
You with your rebel folk songs,
seething under
my dad's jokes
about Semtex,
your rants about Irish oppression
and police brutality, chafed wrists
and bruises
when they let you out.
I wonder
if you've tried to hijack any planes lately,
if your mind and boyish charm have been lost
to the Scotch and red wine.

I do think of you sometimes,
would have stayed in touch,
but for your affair with that madam from work,
whose name I still remember,
the phone echoing eternally into the empty
neglect of your Kilburn bedsit hallway.
You were always a cliché. We were
too young. I would have written,
if you had given up your demons,
your love for me that wasn't really love,
but I no longer have a forwarding address
for the man you sometimes were, once.

In which Malaysia Airlines Flight 133 is not a stagecoach

It's a particular kind of torture at 11,000 feet,
when the kid in the row behind
continually bumps and kicks my seat
and my own children leave pauses between
questions just long enough for me to sink
into sleep, to be jerked up again,

on a flight heading into the future
of the southern hemisphere
when my real trajectory is backward,
to my dad, whose ego needs a scaffold,
to the worn shadow waiting for me
behind my twin,
at her wedding I've had no part in;

a pantomime in which I will be
forever after consigned to play
ugly sister, bloated pumpkin,
never Fairy Godmother,
or her, *God Forbid*. The injustice of it

when the stiletto fits.
I'll plaster on a smile; praying
no one notices it's my eyes that are glass,
and raise champagne to family.

For now, I sit back
in the stale air of the cabin
as a spot begins to pus on my chin.
Despite my lines and increasing grey,
I am a child again.

For all I thought I'd left behind
not a bloody thing has changed.
On touch down the carousel will turn
and turn
in pointless circles
while all my baggage waits to be claimed.

RIP The Brunswick Arms (1837-2006)

You can keep your gastropubs,
your heat lamps, cigars, Armani suits,
chuffing Kir Royales and Thames views;
all we wanted
was her knocked out teeth
and grubby lace;
more foul mouthed
than a Billingsgate fishmonger
but ours.

The summer days of *Stella*,
sausage rolls on paper plates,
Tommy tanked up every Thursday,
butchering *Mack the Knife* on karaoke,
Pointy Pete glaring daggers
at any hapless chancer:
You ain't local mate.
It wouldn't have been the same,
if Laura hadn't been no-nonsense,
no-fools queen behind the bar,
pole faced to strangers
but all sunny-ed up with smiles
for anyone's kid;
if the dogs weren't fixing
baleful eyes on our crisps,
Scottish Chris insisting
the men's lav was haunted,
the boaters in the corner:
John the Light, Sarah flower girl,
Ivan the terribly nice,
The Gwyn Reaper and Buzz

earnestly discussing ropes and tides.
Peeling flock wallpaper,
stale air all fags and piss,
shoved in between the A12,
NF graffiti on Gaselee Street
and the stink of disenchantment.

But sometimes we'd glimpse
the disco ball of the sun
above her flagging heart,
the silent glide of ship masts
sailing on
behind the towers.

Storms

This is why we can't have nice things

It took just weeks to demolish the Bohemia,
the silhouetted ladies writhing around poles
now buried beneath rubble, consigned to the dirt

but I wonder if they will rise in their heels
in the night to dance on the bonnets of cars;
or if they too accepted defeat.

Outside Ferham School a woman boasts
"They won't get me to work, can't mek me".
Aspirations get lost between Steel St and Holmes Lock

as generations draw dole cheques,
forget what it is to bring home a wage;
shame settles and stains like coal dust.

Resignation has been ingrained; trodden
into pavements like the puce in the covered market
loo floors can never quite get clean,

even the river's going nowhere, silted up
with *Farm Foods* plastic bags, *Tennents*
cans, and shopping trolleys – burdens

it can't shake off, while outside The Bridge
the lads are going twos on fags,
waiting for jobs that don't exist.

Midnight. Tesco's car park. A woman
pulls her leopard skin thong down
carcassed thighs, squats between cars for a piss.

Oh they can pretty it up, planting wild
flowers outside the Minster but the playgrounds
are held together with rust, graffiti

and broken glass; bus stops smashed in;
litter bins burnt to shrivelled black
stumps – a generation that believes

this is all they deserve, smash up even
what in the first place wasn't much
with no idea how to get what they want

honestly – austerity just means more of the same.
At a pub across town, in the ladies loo,
a scrawl on a broken window asserts:

this is why we can't have nice things

Those Girls

The ones that mostly
you couldn't get to cross the threshold,
let alone to talk;
the dyed dirty blondes
dead eyes like fish,
the ones who found no refuge in school,
called sket, skank, tramp, bitch;
the ones so beautiful it hurt to look at them,
or fleshy like meat
impaled on skewers that
falls apart on the grill,
the ones so delicate and brittle
they could snap in two,
or who oozed from shouty leggings,
the bravado of crop tops
over half-formed mounds;
the ones caked in make-up, wearing jewellery
they mistook for love,
the silent ones who rarely left home
hidden under veils like shrouds.
Those girls, little more than babbies,
who only need you to listen,
to hold their horror in your hands
like a grenade while they pull the pin,
hold it until your hair and fingertips are singed
and the whole sorry mess explodes
without you letting go.
The ones who push their terror into you
so forcibly the nausea clings
hours after they've gone –
and these are just the ones

who come forward and speak.
Those girls in the 153 pages of the Jay report,
who weren't seen or heard or attended to;
whose hollow '*nos*' won't jump out
from the printed words to echo
in municipal corridors;
whose pleas won't penetrate
the gleaming citadel
of the new council office block,
those girls the EDL want
to fuck all over again – fodder
for their campaign; those girls
and all the others like them
that the baying of media hounds won't soothe;
those girls who everyone failed,
when no one had the stomach
for the petrol-soaked, bloodied edges
of the truth.

Elsie Encounters the EDL

Lunchtimes on Saturdays,
Tesco's car park is *usually always* full
but today there's stacks of room
and there's more police than when
it's just the footie, billions of them.

It's horrible and silent,
like when someone dies;
there's a grey barrier around
the square; like a prison or a castle,
and the police are in a line,
side by side in yellow jackets
but none of them smile.
They've got truncheons and helmets
like at The National Emergency Museum.
Mummy asks a police lady what's going on
then she swears and I tell her off
but I don't stop her
as she grabs my hand
because it all feels wrong.
We walk past ugly red-faced men
holding up England flags,
everyone is in a hurry; my heart beats faster,
and my tummy feels odd.

Mummy says the Muslim boys
aren't having a friendly chat
outside the police station,
she says they've been kettled,
even Lily isn't messing around *for a change*.
How can it be so quiet

when the background is all shouting?
It feels darker than just the sky.
I ask Mummy why
are those men chanting,
punching their fists in the air?

She says those people think
some of your friends shouldn't
be here.

Ferham Park

Stale coke, dog shit, cigarette ends,
the trees underfed,
concrete cracked and deadly
beneath climbing frames,
the playground chip-paper grey
and silent before Sunday tea.

Regeneration didn't make it
over Coronation Bridge, a ghetto
rising a mile from town *No golfing allowed*
states a sign on the grass – *as if!*

Even in the tumbleweed,
everyone stakes their claim,
Graffiti spells out battles more eloquently
than the news: as the *'Chloe luvs Josh'*
and the *'Jade n' Kieran'*s
fade, fresh marker pens
introduce Tomas, Lukas, Nasa.

At the Fun Day in the summer
the Pakistani and Slovak flags
are stolen, the war crystallised
where someone has written:
'english people they are disgusting'
to which, underneath, the inaccurate
reply: *'go home then paki'*

the council's attempts at cohesion
a depressed afternoon of
football, dance, hair braiding
and henna tattoos.

On the roundabout I wait
for the kids to get bored,
watching streets and trees
blur into one like a tired zoetrope.
When we stop

nothing magical has occurred.

Banter

Do you remember the time I visited,
that house in Australia with a pool?
You took swipes at my principles:
Feminist? Shut up!
You so brought me breakfast in bed
in that chalet by Loch Ness,
still kept the photo on top of your TV
– evidence to taunt me with.

That same trip we headed
back from Inverness, giggled
like school girls when you
applied my moisturiser at the bus stop,
flounced down the platform,
tried to catch the train guard's eye,
wanted to share our sleeper cabin with him not me.

In your new life I found you
hefting weights in the gym,
The irony! Look at you, most muscular queen in town!
You shrugged. You loved it over there,
a far cry from Hackney, those Aussie boys
mad for your caramel skin
I'm exotic you preened.

I'd always loved your waspish humour
the arched eyebrow you perfected,
our pantomime of traded insults;
that time I wailed my date
had complained I dressed like a dyke,
your wry grin took in
my dungarees and DM's.

We were always inseparable,
sunny, until that Gold Coast day
you circled the patio with a broom:
Bikini? Really homegirl?!
Keep sweeping houseboy!
flew from my mouth before I knew
what I'd said. A southern breeze
swayed the eucalyptus, my words left
hanging
between
us.

Ode to England, 24th June 2016

You are nothing if not green,
often more duck shit and pond weed
than immaculate borders around lawns.

You plod, you do not dance,
your passivity breath-taking,
your arms flop impotent to your sides,

though your fists are balled.
You tried. You wanted it
to be different, better – we all did.

These days you sell only disappointment,
you are not what you were,
your medals gathering dust,

like a magpie: you bought
your spoils back, they turned to rust
in puddles and our faithful rain.

You're jittery, neighbours unsure whether to stay,
a smiling welcome at the corner shop
but the owner no longer knows his place.

You are side-eyed, petty,
they've got more than me,
the whine of *don't-bother* and apathy,

café windows smeared mildewed pale,
the sallow stoicism of fish and chips,
stolid pork pies, the soggy of ice cream,

endlessly unable to bring home big dreams.
You used to play the big man; you are
now spectacular in your tendency to fail;

underdog, a Victoria sandwich that sunk,
a tumble in the three-legged race –
never a team player, you never learned to share.

We remain here with you. Or bail.

Baptism

They don't tell you

that the echoes of moans on your ante-natal trip to the Whitechapel will hit the pit of what is left of your stomach with a thud.

They don't tell you what birth trauma feels like; you understand it by the student midwife asking: "Why won't she stop crying?" When they take you back to the very room you were in last time after the failed home birth, where for five hours straight they told you not to push when every sinew of your body screamed to do nothing but.

They won't have said that going for a walk round the hospital grounds alone is a bad idea when the pain comes all in a rush and you cling to walls hand over hand wishing you weren't too proud to ask for help or that making it back didn't feel like scaling a mountain of glass.

They won't know that the smell of Pink Grapefruit shower gel will forever after make your breathing snag or that it is a mistake to accept the loan of a copy of 'Take a Break' from the woman in the bed opposite as the horror stories only accentuate your mounting agony.

They don't point out how ridiculous you will feel bouncing on a birthing ball however much distress you are in or that the midwives might forget to examine you so you only just make it to the labour ward at 8cm.

They don't mention the poo you might accidentally squeeze out on the antiseptic floor or that for the second and hopefully last time in your life you will be utterly incapable of speech or coherent thought.

They forget to say that if you deliver too late in the day you may miss dinner and the café will be shut after 16 hours of labour when mostly all you did was throw up and shit.

They don't tell you that at first you may not recognise this tiny alien as your own or that padding along the corridor to the phone the day after she arrived with her on your arm is frowned upon and apparently you should have left her in her cot to cry.

They will leave out the bit where they give your baby back in a blood stained towel or how the floor of the loo will never quite disguise the remains of other women's discharges or that in the depth of night when you have now been awake for 32 hours straight and counting the girl in the next bed will ask you to breastfeed her baby when the only milk you yourself have produced is a pathetic dribble.

They neglect to tell you that from this point on you will cry uncontrollably at adverts and never again watch the french subtitled films you used to love.

They tell you your life will never be the same but they don't tell you how.

They don't tell you half the stuff that might be more fucking useful than watching a plastic doll being pushed through a prosthetic pelvis or that nearly nine years on all this will still have the immediacy of a punch.

Or that the responsibility remains more terrifying than you dare admit.

It wouldn't make a scrap of difference if they did.

Welcome to Scarborough YHA

I know how to make friends
Lily says; *first you smile,*
if they smile back, it's a start.

Amongst crowded book spines,
piled high board games,
stray pieces slot in,

it's an oddly wholesome sharing,
the dance of strangers
around the toaster,

the well-behaved
tyranny of quiet children,
the smiles of cardigan girls.

We are nomads, scavengers in
the sand, rewarded by golf balls,
a trinket box, a picture in a bin,

though the real prize
is the deserted beach after rain,
the sea a rare glittering thing.

It opens me; I am all breath,
dancing steps and air.
The kids are magnets for life,

while I am the tide going out,
folding into solitude
after their bedtime.

And this is why I came,
held by pen and paper,
mugs of tea, the seduction

of cubby holes, long distance trucks,
nothing but a bunk, a kettle,
hardly room to stretch;

silence, a book lit by a single lamp,
pared back into myself.

Sunday Morning at Kite Kite Falls, Piha

Forgive me, I didn't
go to church today
but pilgrimaged through trees,
palm leaves bent in supplication,
a dripping canopy of praise.
I found the pool's cool benediction,
prayed through the waterfall
speechless in its gasp,
the lift of a cold so sharp,
I braced in its absolution.

My limbs beneath the
surface candle-pale,
a chancel of rocks
that looks from above, as tiny
and insubstantial as pebbles
yet wholly and infinitely itself.

A moment I couldn't
find at an altar
or kneeling in a pew.
Afterwards, I warmed my faith
with a towel, gratitude.

The Way the Words Were

Sometimes you chose to toss them into the air,
to dance thin as paper butterflies,
waited to see which flowers they'd grace.
Tested their weight, as if worth
could be determined by scales,
held them close or cradled them like shells.
It was never an exact science
yet some were as snug as glass slippers
but much more comfortable.
Some came out in a rat-a-tat
of machine gun fire, bullets
that couldn't be recalled;
the sheer force of a waterfall,
that sped and gushed. So even
rocks were worn and smoothed.
Maybe they were ointments or herbs
with the power to heal, if only you knew
how to pick the ones you needed.
There were days when there was nothing
left on the shelves – not even candles or prayers
remained; or a surfeit you decided not to use,
kept them in your pockets like pebbles.
They could do no damage there.
You were never once tempted
to give them up; the ones you did not
voice, you wrote down.
It was always a love affair.

Tribe

My people strip the flesh from bone,
leave only what is honed, necessary.

They blister their fingers in a frenzy
of capture, prefer to hunt alone.

They are silent, they watch,
they're here though you don't heed them;

thieves who steal the contents
of your mouth if it pleases them,

trap what others don't value
stalk their prey as long as it takes,

they are patient, they wait.
Invisible, my people creep,

forage, grab morsels, tend seeds,
wrap their children in lullabies,

whisper to soothe. They are
no different from you,

they listen, nothing is wasted.
Even dreams are prevented escape.

My people arm themselves with paper
sling arrows, catch metaphors in their nets,

they are fishermen with ears for hooks,
they trawl the depths for bounty

haul it up, parade it proudly.
My people feast on words and are sated.

They pummel and pound ideas
until they beat with a life of their own.

My people are conjurors,
midwives, warriors, gardeners.

As dusk gathers so will they,
to huddle round fires and share.

We can be found in the flicker of flames
drawn in close. Join us.

On Finding Myself at the Gates of Hell

As it happens, I never see
the inside of Court Room Four,
our barristers settle in the corridors
and waiting rooms.

It's hot, so very hot,
my trousers – cheap, synthetic
– stick to the seats.

The wigs and robes sit opposite
men in designer jeans
with knocked out teeth,
grey pallor from the fags;

the young lads awkward
with stiff suits, brittle hair,
who share cheeky banter – first
name terms with their counsel.

A man leaves;
"only eight counts, not bad"
his companion stares in disbelief.
It's so damn hot.

The whirr of a mechanical fan
keeps going off,
insinuates itself inside my head.
The wait is eternal;

time I can't use –
desperate for a wee,

but too scared to move
in case I get called

the sun a blister
that burns and burns.

Immersion

In Deep

You are never indifferent;
it is always a case of how and when,
not if. You want the shock of him,
the affront, the tussle – to succumb,
to be as one, engulfed, submerged.

His skin is dappled,
sun-dimpled; the copper ore
of the hills pours down
pooling over pebbles
to kiss his chest,
the rest is shadowed,
cast hunter-green
by the dip and lift of leaves
from trees that hug the bank.

You know better,
he is neither tame, nor kind.
It's not why you came here
but it doesn't hold you back.

You live for summers like this,
to surrender to the dance,
the tingle, the abandon.
Sure-footed, you offer yourself,
wade in.

Perhaps in a past life
you had scales, a flash of tail.

He is chameleon,
never gives a straight answer.
You see right through him;
it doesn't matter.
You let him have you,
gulp you whole,
you don't say no.

Wedding Hymn

How sticky and clinging,
how un-English the weather
as darkness clothed the hotel
and you slid your fingers
in my lacy knickers
as I brushed my teeth
in the honeymoon suite;
the wallpaper tearing itself to get free,
the pipes singing
their own noisy praise.

Anniversary

In our thirteenth year,
I try to suppress my superstition
yet when I dropped
the beach-stone heart
I keep on the kitchen shelf,
it cracked in two. I haven't got round

to gluing it back together.

The tea I make
tastes of impatience;
you only say sorry as a protest
when you're not.

But we should congratulate ourselves
that we're still here;
the suspicion you might leave
wraps itself
like the tangled grasp
of seaweed round my heart,
despite the boomerang
you placed
over the bedroom door;
the shell of your Triumph Tiger
gathering dust;
you are the anchor now
to all my peaks and troughs.

And if ours has been
a shore of stones
to walk barefoot across,

all the sharp edges of us
are soft and worn as sea glass.
The waves' smash the breakers,
smooth away splinters
until the threat of injury fades.
This weathering
of shadow days and sun,
tells me we will go on
standing, long after
each storm has passed.

Anchorage

Counting the days
on the shores of inland hills,
gazing out across terraces,
piled clumsy as lobster pots,
streets strung like lines across bows
pavements slick as oil in the rain,
I wait, heavy with this child
who each day tightens
her hold on my skin made taut
as the fibres of a net
cast out, now full;

my man is homebound,
charting through shipping lanes
with a skipper who sees
no use for maps and flares,
is careless with ropes
and once, at night cast off, navigated
by a passing ship, to find by dawn
he'd hugged the shoreline,
following the headlights of a truck
on the coast road.

They make passage from Ostend,
fighting waves of sickness,
the retched proximity,
hemmed in
by hours of vast insipid grey,
surrendered to swells of indifference.

So when at last he docks
and I have waddled my return to berth,
he leads me on board where I despair
for this vessel so unprepared to be a home,
only stubborn dryness from the taps
exposed electric cables,
and days from arriving,
our water baby who has learnt too soon
the art of waiting.

The Thames men read the wind
and tides, bring the cauls of angel births
on deck for luck, for they know
nothing involving water
can ever be trusted.

Not until she is here,
calm, harboured in my arms,
can I breathe.
We no longer need an anchor;
we always keep one near.

Dear Canal

Thank you for returning our youngest – twice!
She has no sense of danger as you know
but was grateful not to encounter crocodiles.
Also for spitting out our cat,
grumpy and bedraggled though she was,
that was a nice touch; she'll learn.
If this winter you could
keep the freezing to a minimum
that would be appreciated,
and leave the hosepipe flowing at least?
We don't need much.
Please continue to cradle our home
in your slippery embrace.
Although we know you are still harbouring
knives, forks and spoons,
two pairs of glasses, the cordless drill
and a mobile phone, hold them;
we'll live without those.

Treading Water at Hathersage Lido

Equanimity is the smell of chlorine,
ripples breaking over my hands
that I push like prayers
into forbidding clouds that clamp
all the edges down,
seamlessly glued to the hills.
I am bereft of blue sky,
the water artificial, a riviera hue,
its clasp fools me
into a pretence of warmth.
Hathersage pool reminds me
of the glacier beauty of your eyes,
all the places we swam,
our friendship that you let slip
beneath the waves to drown.

Sea Level

She will slap you down,
pick you up, spit you out
thump you on the back
until your only reply is down,
knees pitted and grazed
by shale and grit;
she will let you rise
only long enough
to throw you from your feet,
punch the breath from your lungs,
remind you, you can never win.

And yet, today she smiles;
lulls you with waves
lapping soft as a cat's tongue,
touches your toes in a shy hello,
gives you the surprise of starfish
shells as perfectly translucent
as a baby's fingernails,
enfolds you in the vast arc of her arms,
under a sky stretching to contain the world.

You hear her in the whisper
and the crash; *This is life child.*

Deluge

Deluge

The sky
is a steel sheet
riveted over the door
of a repossessed flat.
Our car on the way home
is battered, as gusts threaten to
swerve us into the outside lane, rain
hits the windscreen leaving marks like
cigarette burns before they dissipate. We are
cocooned, blinded, stunned by the force; but we've
survived worse. Like last summer, when the canal's level rose
ever closer to the lock gates, all twelve foot of them, putting our trust
in ballast and ropes, the three in the morning checks. I didn't anticipate I'd spend
my life fighting or that abundance could be this depriving as the rain continued
to fall and fall, only ever down. At primary school my teacher called me stoic
(she meant stubborn) I was the kind of child who refused to go out to play;
if she made me, I took my book to a bench. Five years in the north
we have been deluged, swamped; by bills, demands,
increasing costs, as the water outside oblivious
to us creeps higher, finds the gaps. Cheap boots
didn't last the winter, the damp seeps into my
toes, the hatches leak onto the beds.
In this decade, it's not about us
anymore, a flood would take
the children too if we let it.
If we didn't keep bailing out,
scraping by, paying
with hours,
tired eyes,
prayers.

Where they burn books...

"That was but a prelude; where they burn books, they will ultimately burn people also."

Heinrich Heine, 1933, Germany.

Off Ferham Rd, the terraces are
pimpled with satellite dishes, scarred
by boarded windows, broken glass
doors are open to the street laying the innards bare,
kameez and jeans lift in the breeze
on a rash of washing lines; garish flags
over unloved streets. Gangs of no one's
children, with grubby faces and wide grins
gather round the prize
of an abandoned buggy,
a discarded tyre,
the latest influx is Slovakian; kids
stopping in an outbreak of stares when we pass,
they don't ask, they know.

We also don't belong.

In America Pastor Terry Jones threatens
to burn 100 copies of the Q'uran;
the English Defence League invites him to the U.K.

December 2010 on Channel Four news,
an Imam from the Luton mosque attended
by the Stockholm bomber, in muted tones,
despairs "Could I have done more?
could I have got alongside him?
His words were of extremity, but not terrorism.
I challenged all his distorted views of Islam
and thought that was the end of it."
but on ITN and in The Sun, it's only bombs.

At home, another match is held to a box,
as the body of Laura Wilson is found
floating in the canal at Holmes,
half a mile from my daughter's primary.
Neighbours who've lived here over a generation
don't speak the language of belonging;
going to school together didn't breed trust.
An unholy marriage of Jeremy Kyle
and X Factor Saturdays with Asian hip hop
and Al Jazeera, a tension that predates Laura's murder;

if she had only stayed quiet
about the married man she slept with
who might just see her as any slag kuffar
looking for a way out, any girl
who thought a baby would make him neglect family,
culture and Allah – but she wasn't one of the chosen ones,
the few English girls in eastern dress, chubby
brown boys on their hips.

So even if his guilt was no more than lust,
he added more volumes to the blaze, more
excuses;

because the BNP will get hold of this,
will twist this ugly crime into votes,
will offer her family a plasma TV, new carpets
for upstairs; poverty, fury and grief
a heady mix; the streets electric
as emotions crackle and spit.

'Do not cross' tape hatches by the canal, outside school
I keep my head down,

silence pools between small groups
that words cannot bridge,
comments muttered behind hands clog the air,
fat white girls with prams
stub out their fags, chivvy their kids,
Pakistani men strut
from their Toyotas, Nissans.
I don't get the nuances, just
trying to find a place to fit round here.
But Urdu slang in school books gets scribbled over,
some Yorkshire lasses cover old tattoos with a veil,
swap nights on the beer for a demure piety.

At the school Nativity
more than half the school are Muslim,
reciting the Christmas story.
It seems odd to make them.
I'm grateful when Sky's mum sits next to me
until she complains that Sky,
with a tea towel round her head
is being turned into a paki.
My shocked silence must seem complicit
to the Asian mums in the row behind
as a time-honoured school tradition
becomes something more malign.

And I think I can hear the scrape of a match,
the whisper of sacred pages
as the flames begin to catch.

The Flood

Yes, we are worried
about the rivers, portentous
against our doors,
scrambling over the tops of our boots;
boredom is very underrated.
But we will not be manic, we will be stolid,
we will eschew despair and panic
despite this falling away.

Oh, for the days when we were unafraid
for our lives and those of others,
when the year's tides did not bring
a shelling of bodies,
boats with a clamour of precious,
become dead weight,
treated to a welcome of
indifference, hate, closed doors.

No one thought the same waters
would invade our villages,
stumble over the cobbles
like a heaving stampede,
bringing the sick mud reek of ruin,
colour leached from postcard pretty
to sepia, the prayers of toss-turn nights,
rash deciding about what to save.

In the end there's nothing cups of tea
a hug, or tins of beans can't ease;
as humanity mucks in, mops up,
some Muslim, some Israeli,

and with the flowers appeased,
the carpets wrung out,
the washing lines hung;
some sense of being righted.

Kyrie Eleison, Christe Eleison,
united against engulfment or breaches
leaks or holes, we'll take comfort
once more in symbols –
perhaps a dove, an olive branch.

Drowning

When the news breaks and the tide cannot be turned
I find comfort in the Muslim call to prayer on TV,
its mathematical calm laps over me
like today as I paint, ripples of chatter
from the Eastern European family fishing
on the opposite bank of the canal.
I relax into the peace of incomprehensible words
the laughter of children – still the same –
the cheers when they catch a fish.
I wouldn't eat anything from this water
maybe they wouldn't either,
I push my assumptions down, drown them in paint.

We co-exist in this subdued day
Cloud muffling out any extremes
the odd phrase in English reaches me
and when they leave, a man calls out:
Beautiful painting- you come paint my house?
See you next time!

Not everything can be covered, made new.
When my friend's appeal for asylum was refused
I went round, the nakedness of the packing boxes
the panic in her daughters' eyes
and her without her hijab.
Somehow I couldn't hug her
seeing her so exposed.
Three years later they let her stay.

Isn't that all anyone wants,
a safe place to call home?

I go back to painting,
the grey green expanse grows,
soothing my eyes. If only
it didn't remind me of the cold sea,
the slip slop of the brush like the slap of waves
lifting a dress to expose a nappy
breaking over pliable limbs,
on her head a swirl of dark curls
frames her little face,
as if in repose.

Containment

He says there are three things

that always look worse than
they are; water, oil and blood.

Which may be true,
but the river shouldn't
insinuate its way inside our hull,

puddling on the floor, blooming
febrile tendrils into concrete.
We're not so naïve as to suppose
there won't be some, or why have bilges?

So far it is a trickle not a flood,
a dim maze revealed,
puzzling through crevices
stubborn against the mop
that even as I wring it out

the floor pattern grows darker,
like a negative in the fixing bath
or those magic pictures
the kids used to have,
where brushing with water
called forth rainbows.

There are no portents now,
he has been waist deep in the grey of the canal
sticking Milliput into rivet holes
like the Dutch boy at the dam;

his heroics stem nothing.
But we're not going down just yet;
It could take weeks, or months.

Steel was supposed to hold.
It isn't the big things that capsize us
It is the creep, the slowfall,
the peck peck peck violence
of the dripping tap, the seep
of our youth a tide going out,
the balloon puncture of sorry,
drowning in an old friend's silence.

Who doesn't need to feel held,
contained by a vessel
without holes, however small;
no one needs the kind of life
that leaks like a sieve,
no more so than when,
tortoise-shelled,
we carry our home with us
and live on water.

Thank you for buying *Deluge*. It is Charlotte Ansell's third poetry collection with us; we hope you enjoyed it. We certainly did! We have been publishing Charlotte's work since 2002 and after seventeen years she remains one of our favourite poets.

—§—

the waterways series publishes full collections of poetry under the banner of flipped eye publishing, a small publisher dedicated to publishing powerful new voices in affordable volumes. Founded in 2001, flipped eye has won awards and international recognition through a focus on publishing fiction and poetry that is clear and true, rather than exhibitionist.

If you would like more information about flipped eye publishing, please join our mailing list online at www.flippedeye.net.